# THE FIRST BOOK OF LAST TIMES

Written by Ron Wiggins

Cartoons by Pat Crowley

*To our loved ones*

THANKS FOR SPECIAL HELP to:
Cynthia Glocker, Mary McLachlin, Jan
Norris, Ken Walters, Jay Ziglinski and
Alan Zlotky; and thanks also to family
and friends who kept us on task by never
failing to ask, "How's the book coming?"

# CONTENTS

# Foreword

As we blaze our separate paths through life, we are inclined to notch certain memories — the first times — which serve as historic markers along the way.

We seldom take note of the last times, perhaps because when they occur we have no way of knowing they will not happen again. But these events are every bit as significant as the first times, for they are transitions, marking our passage from one stage of our development to the next.

In *The First Book of Last Times,* author Ron Wiggins and cartoonist Pat Crowley retrace the route from infancy and find these universal points of reference that link us all: the last time Dad carried you from the back seat of the car up to bed; the last time you sat on the kitchen chair and wondered if your legs would ever be long enough for your feet to touch the floor; the last time Mom wet her fingers on her tongue and pasted down your cowlick.

One of the perils of growing up is that we put away not only our childish things, but our childlike things as well — our innocence, our emotions, our unique perpective on the world. We cram it all into a closet in the mansion of our mind and lock it up. In time we forget where we put the key. Wiggins and Crowley have found it and opened the door.

*The First Book of Last Times* is a book you will never finish, for when you are through reading, the joyous, poignant memories of other last times will come tumbling out of your mental closet to fascinate and entertain you.

— Richard Des Ruisseaux, columnist for *The Courier-Journal,* Louisville, Ky.

There was, of course, a last time you were carried sleeping from the car.

The occasion was neither celebrated nor remarked unless your dad said something like:

"Holy cow! This kid's a moose. From now on he walks."

And so you did. The next time your folks came in late, your dad squeezed your shoulder and shook you gently, saying, "We're home. Wake up. Let's go." And obligingly, you trundled into the house, bouncing off furniture and walls until you crawled into bed where somebody later came and undressed you and tucked you in and perhaps pressed lips against your cheek.

There was a last time for that, too. And a last time anybody tied a shoe for you or made you use the booster board at the barber shop, or gave you money knotted up in a handkerchief or told you to look both ways or close your mouth while you're eating, and on and on and on.

That's what this book is about: Last times. The closing of hundreds of personal epochs, each one un-noted and uncelebrated. Well, why not first times? There was a first time you left the house in your Sunday best without your mom wetting a handkerchief with her tongue and scrubbing a dirt spot and a freckle or two off your face, and there was a first time you went off the high dive and a first time you rode a bicycle without training wheels.

Sorry, our hearts go out to last times precisely because they sneak by us. We know you can remember that first time you went head-first off the high dive. You can remember the commitment and mental rehearsals that took, how very much farther away the water looked from above than it did from the base of the ladder, how you crouched and bent over so as to make the water come closer, the jeers from the other kids behind you and finally the point of no return as you toppled forward, the rush of wind and the sting of water ram-injected up your nose even as your eyeballs were crushed against the back of your skull.

The fun stuff you remember.

But do you remember that last craven incident in your high-board career when you chickened out and jumped? Or worse, the last time you thought you would jump off the high board, took one look and climbed down the ladder in disgrace, against traffic, while 10 other kids despised you for a coward?

We can fetch these priceless moments back for you, but as Strother Martin said in "Cool Hand Luke," you've got to get your mind right. Take this test. When you see a waxed floor, what's the first thing you think of?

If you said wax buildup, you are much too grown up for your own good and you need help and you've come to the right place. You should have said sliding in your socks. When you were a kid you immediately recognized a waxed floor for the only thing they're good for which is sliding in your socks.

You took off your shoes, got a running start and slid. Talk about fun. It was good exercise. It was exciting. You could have contests. It wore out your socks. We here at this book still slide in our socks.

"If you're in there wearing out your socks, I'll wear you out," your mother said.

When's the last time your mother said, "If I have to come in there one more time, I'm going to wear you out?"

Childhood and growing up wasn't all fun. It was kind of a soap opera. In fact, that's why people watch soap operas, because in a weird kind of way people miss the rich and dramatic lives they knew in

their childhood. Whatever the rewards and stresses of adult life, it's a millpond compared to your basic tempest-tossed kid life.

Consider. You start life perfectly sensitive to pain and humiliation, but without the least idea of how to avoid either. You are dropped defenseless into an environment teeming with huge people empowered to snatch you up and stash you in bed without dessert. On the brighter side, the fun you had playing hide-and-seek at dusk makes an adult's week at Club Med seem like a lecture on bauxite imports by comparison.

When was the last time you carefully gauged the distance of the person who was "it" from the base, chose your moment and then sprinted desperately to the base, beating the kid by a half-step? You don't remember. But there was such a time, and when you went home in the cool of that fall evening, it never occurred to you to think:

"That was my last hide-and-seek game. After this moment, I am too old. Millions of children will play that game from now until God closes his book on humankind, but for me, this game is no more. The next time I give any thought to this game,

it will be to say, 'Yes, you can play after supper, but if you're not in by 8 o'clock, I'm going to wear you out.'"

Set your brain on "retrieve" and see if you can place these last times in your life:

● You let someone wiggle your tooth — *"Not too much! Not too much!"*

● You were under orders to eat vegetables of various hue and learned to hide, redistribute and otherwise palm food with a dexterity to baffle The Great Blackstone.

● There was no such thing as too sweet and you put sugar on your Frosted Flakes®.

● You had rocking chair races until you were screamed at.

● You were congratulated for the fine job you did on pulling the silk out of the corn on the cob. Won similar accolades for the fury of your onslaught with a potato masher.

● You begged to lick the pancake batter bowl, convinced it had to be the same as licking a cake bowl, and your mom said, "Okay, but you'll be sorry" and you were. Along with dyed Easter eggs, file this under "major disappointments" of your lifetime.

● You were fascinated by the cow inside the can inside the can inside the can on the Pet® evaporated milk can and wondered if it went on forever.

21, 22, 23,
24, 25, 26, 27,
28, 29, 30, 31, 32,
33, 34, 35, 36,
37, 38...

Babyhood is a kaleidoscope of last times, galloping phases, revolving door stages, peekaboo, droopy diapers, gummy zwieback and open-mouth baby kisses.

Especially gummy zwieback open-mouth baby wet kisses by ambush.

You used to do this to people. You were 18 months old, at large in the living room, armed with zwieback clutched in your fat, grubby little fist. And you were in a great mood, an expansive mood because you had gotten the hard toast where you wanted it, slick with mouth slime and pliable.

Suddenly, you felt like sharing. And behold! — dead ahead across the room was a slumbering adult on the sofa, face at your level. You liked that face. It was your dad's face, slack-jawed and snoring. You went at that face full toddle and jammed your toast in that face while planting your trademark open mouth wet baby kiss on his whiskery cheek.

Yes, you did that out of love. And there was a last time for it, too, which in truth may have also been the first time. Sometimes major events coincide on account that fathers are so overwhelmed by such spontaneous displays of generosity that from then on, they nap with their faces to the backrest.

Nobody can possibly keep up with baby last times, no, not even when they

are fervently anticipated, as in the last time you were colicky and had to be held and walked during choice sleeping hours. If you are still a walker of babies, consider the next time you are on active duty, stumbling in your exhaustion, that these things end; one night you will be walking and patting and thinking you have been walking babies forever, and will forevermore.

And wrong you will be as usual. Life changes and on that very night you will be walking your crying baby for the last time, perhaps only weeks away from your last whiff of Johnson & Johnson® baby powder.

Put these in your memory stereoscope and see if you can relive the last time:

● You ran flank speed to your mother with your arms outstretched and raised to be picked up. Which poses a profound philosophical question here. How was it decided that you would no longer be picked up? Was it because you no longer flew to mommy, hands raised for the hoist? Or was it because the last 20 times you did so, mom said, "Forget it, the kid's a moose" and you finally gave up?

● You were tossed. Dads and uncles did this while your mom screamed like a wounded thing. Tossing was a thrill that the designers of The Cyclone at Coney Island wished to duplicate. In fact, all thrill seeking, whether it be skiing, surfing, skydiving and stock-car racing, are

19

but futile quests to relive that thrill you knew when your daddy tossed you three feet above his head and caught you by the simple act of impaling your armpits with his thumbs.

Time out— there was one more thrill that was fellow to the toss and so important as to qualify as a Cheap Thrill (Chapter 6). Curb swinging. It worked like this: while crossing the street, your parents stood on either side of you, grasping your hands. As they neared the curb, they stepped out ahead of you and then with perfect timing, swung you up to the curb, achieving a perfect parabolic arc that gave you that elevator-dropping sensation in your stomach as you lighted on the sidewalk.

(But, of course, there was a last time you were curb-swung and while the thrill may have receded into the misty past, it is remembered and pursued by jetsetters in their $60,000 Porsches and quarter-million dollar ocean racers.)

● You teethed on the dog's bone.

● You availed yourself of the miniature beach-in-a-box that you shared with the cat.

● You were peekabooed. Again, these stage-ending mechanisms are imperfectly understood if they are understood at all. To restate the question: Are we genetically programmed to sense that moment when it is no longer apposite to

say, "Baby all gone (in mock dismay) . . . PEEKABOO!" Or is it the baby who informs us that the game is over by no longer laughing? In either case, no baby is peekabooed after his time.

● You were piggied and weeweeweed all the way home.

● You were rolly-pollied (which rite specifies an adult towering over Baby, with index finger over Baby's tummy, which digit is descending menacingly in a tight spiral, culminating in the thrill-horror of that kamikaze belly-button plunge as the maniac adult cries, "Rolly-polly, rolly-polly, gonna tickle-that-baby-in-the-tummy!").

(We must here call another sociologi-cal time out to expound our twin theories that all theater and literature proceeds from "This little piggy" while the horror film industry is essentially rolly-polly re-visited.)

● You were fed mashed peas (we have another theory propounding a caus-al relationship between force-feeding in-fants mashed peas and adult criminal behavior).

● You carried around your potty, showed it off to company and offered demonstrations.

● You were being held and decided to visit someone else by diving out of the arms of the holder with no notice whatso-ever to either party.

Brothers and sisters.

If you neglected to have brothers and sisters you not only missed out on a world of satisfaction and a galaxy of grief, you'll get about as much nostalgia out of this chapter as a captive spouse at a class reunion. So what are we supposed to do — *not* talk about siblings just so you won't feel left out?

All right, nobody's making you read this chapter. It's not on the test. You were probably spoiled anyway, what with no hand-me-downs and about a billion uncles and aunts and grandparents going crazy trying to figure out what to give you on grand occasions since your parents had already spoiled you beyond redemp-tion with a 12-foot giraffe from FAO Schwarz.

To begin at the beginning as we understand it, the universe exploded and swirled and cooled and came equipped with hydrogen and carbon and oxygen just so that it could produce you at the end of about 20 billion years. But the universe, besides being annoyingly intricate, also tends to redundancy which is why you ended up with brothers and sisters under your roof.

At least that's how it was with us.

For now we will omit gender and speak only in terms of little sibs and big sibs. Little sibs were for following you around, tattling, getting into your stuff and crying

23

at the least little punch on the shoulder. They had their points, which were: they made excellent guinea pigs ("Tell me if this hurts"), they could be framed, stashed in right field, terrified by a Technicolor® description of The Thing Under Their Bed, snuck away from, and used as an excuse to go trick-or-treating when you were too old ("No, I don't mind taking Billy through the neighborhood, honest I don't").

Big sibs were dangerous, mean, treacherous, stingy, Monopoly® cheaters, allowed to do anything, independent and thought they were hot stuff. In their favor, they had interesting things in their drawers and closets, were fun to spy on, usually stuck with the grueling jobs, namely dish washing, lawn mowing, weeding and vacuuming. Best of all, they were the shock troops that fought your parents for freedoms and curfews you would enjoy years later with an easy insouciance to make your eldest sib resent both you and your parents for years.

You went through stages and out of stages with your brothers and sisters before you realized you were in the midst of them, much less that your "last times" were slamming shut the doors of your childhood like wind gusting through the house. Let's reflect on a few.

There was a last time you:

● Were told what would happen to you

if you woke up that baby.

● Succumbed to misty thoughts of the good old days and sought to relive them by asking your mom for a taste of your little brother's or sister's strained plums.

● Watched your mom spoon strained spinach down your little sib's throat and gagged at the very idea of it.

● Broke an older sib's precious model which you had only borrowed and now had to put the pieces back where you found them, trying to make it look *not* broken and then, sick at your stomach at the horror of what you had done, mentally rehearsed a defense built on the pathetic premise that you never touched it and, besides, it was already broken when

you picked it up.

● Heard the crunch of gravel in the driveway, meaning that your mom was back from shopping much earlier than she had any right to be and here's your little sister crying over a love tap that no jury in the world would convict you for if they but knew how aggravating she could be.

● Were pushed in a grocery cart by a big brother or sister who could really show you a good time except when you hit the pyramid of Stokely® green beans.

● Talked a little brother into curling up into an old tire for an exciting roll down the hill and later on had no choice really but to tell your mother that the

child was obviously dazed by the crash and that you had not encouraged him in his folly, quite the contrary, had expressly warned him against it, and that the next thing you knew, there he was bouncing merrily down the hill while you watched helpless and horrified.

● Your dad said, "Hey, you kids pipe down in there!" Dads who had served in the military were full of that kind of talk. "Belay that." "On the double." "Make it snappy." "Stow it." "If I have to come in there, I'm lowering the boom."

● Raced a sibling for the best seat and if you lost it, went directly to appellate court petitioning for relief on an equity plea, recalling that complainant had been denied the front seat (or best chair) last time.

● Feasted at a family gathering seated at a card table with the other kids and were thrilled to be away from the adults where you could have a good time blowing bubbles in your milk without some huge person whacking you on the wrist.

● Were humiliated at a family feast by being forced to sit with "the little kids" and were so incensed that you barely ate a helping of everything and most certainly didn't give them the satisfaction of hearing you beg for seconds on dessert. Anyway, it worked and next year there you were, taking your place at the big table within wrist-slapping distance of 10 stuffy grown-ups.

Your transition from home to grade school was trans-galactic. Your imagination tried to prepare you for the immensity of it but failed because no matter how grandly school was touted, here was the bottom line:

*Mom won't be there. They won't even let her ride the bus.*

What if you got lost on that very first day and couldn't find your room and you were doomed to wander forever down The Hallway of Lost Children? Your mom gave you lunch money and cautioned you not to lose it. But what if you did? What then?

*"I'm sorry, but since you cannot seem to keep up with your lunch money, we have no choice but to put you at a table by yourself where you will starve and die and be an example to others."*

School thrilled and frightened you. There is no overstating the role it played in your life. Indeed, T.L. Freeman, reporting in *The Journal of Irreproducible Results,* concluded that since *apparent* time (that is, time as you actually experience it) is longer the younger you are, you have actually lived 51 percent of your life by the time you are 10 years old.

(Troy determined that only at age 20

does a calendar year *seem* like a year. Thus, at age 7 a year seems like four years, and at age 50 a year seems like three and a half months.)

But we digress from the focus of this whole book which is that we go through many phases, each with its characteristic behavior, rituals, rites, agonies and ecstasies. And as surely as the bounciest seat is at the very back of the school bus, each phase is closed forever by a last time, unremarked and slighted to memory.

We mean are we right about how you were willing to trade a cinnamon red-hot jawbreaker for that bucking bronco ride in that very last seat, especially when the bus bounced over unpaved roads? And of course, you can't quite put your finger on that last time — what was it, sixth grade — or even tenth grade during that last field trip.

There was a last field trip, too, but it's lost in your brain somewhere.

It's sad somehow, because last times are not noted at all, much less remembered, but we're going to reflect on them anyway, dig them up a shard at a time until we've reconstructed something that looks and feels and smells a lot like your childhood.

There was a last time you drew a house with curly smoke coming out of the chimney, a house shone upon by a yellow sun with yellow rays, put there with your yellowest crayon. You were an artist then and knew how to put apples on trees and color them red and almost stay within the lines. You prized a sharp crayon and despised those waxy octagonal crayons which would get a grain of sand under the point and make your skin crawl when it scraped the paper.

You confidently drew self-portraits in those days and labeled them, lest there be any doubt, "Me."

Naps were a very important part of your early years and were generally written into teacher's contracts. There was a last time you took your nap rug to school. After that naps were taken at desks, sometimes after recess, sometimes after lunch when it was thought that a quiet period would help you digest your food.

There was a last time in late May that you lay your head flat against your desk and sweated and felt your head slide inexorably down the desk top as you inhaled the sharp aroma of wood and varnish. How many times did you let your pencil roll down and then blow it uphill

to fall back into its groove? When was the last time you did that?

School was the cafeteria, the crash of bins of tableware hoisted by hefty, sweating, kindly women with hairnets and starchy white uniforms. Much of the food was suspect, unrecognizable and just plain unappetizing. Remember that gloppy hamburger stew (to call it something) that had peas imbedded in it?

Funny, we call it dog food, too.

And just about the time you decided to bring your lunch they had sloppy joes and peanut-butter cookies, the kind lovingly impressed with fork crisscrosses.

*"Too bad you missed school yesterday. We had hamburgers and butterscotch squares."*

You wanted so badly that gold star after your name for eating all of your lunch that you gagged and swallowed the pickled beets and tried not to throw up and did throw up and didn't get the star although the rule should have stated that if you tried so hard you threw up, you should get the star anyway.

There was a last time you bartered your extra milk for somebody else's fruitcup. There was a last time you kept your eyes open against cornbread poachers.

Did you ever dip the paper sanitary cover of your Sweetheart® straw into butter and blow it to the ceiling where it stuck? Kind of reminds us of those last three swats in the dean of boys' office, doesn't it?

When was the last time you "s(he) loves-me-s(he)-loves-me-not-ed" with a straw? We're betting it was before plastic straws ended that, sending all the loves-me-loves-me-not trade back to the daisies.

One last lunchroom last time — ice cream cups. Did you eat yours hard, wolfing it down for a crippling behind the eyeball headache, or stir it up with your little wooden spoon? It actually tasted better stirred. . . . Hey, we're serious, it *actually* tasted better. . . . No, it is not our imagination and we'll bet you a million dollars that if you take 100 people and blindfold them and let them taste hard ice cream and ice cream from the same batch all whipped up, most of them will prefer the soft. . . . Well, of course, "prefer" is the same as "tastes better." . . . You know we're right and won't admit it. Okay, we'll bet you a *million* million dollars. . . .

School was also recess. There used to be a psychological test that asked you if you liked the game of drop the handkerchief. What would that tell about you? It would tell the shrinks whether you were a popular child. Popular children loved drop the hanky because they remember the excitement of picking up that handkerchief and chasing the dropper around the circle. But if your schoolmates didn't like you, you just remember the hopelessness of waiting and never being chosen. It was a dumb game and you hated it.

There was a last time you played drop the handkerchief and red rover. *"Red Rover, Red Rover, send Patsy right over."* Small-for-their age kids loved red rover because the other side picked the lightest opponent to dash full speed into the hand-holders in an attempt to break through the chain. Red rover was such an exciting game that the concept lived and evolved and was institutionalized so that the excitement might continue through adulthood. That institution is known as the National Football League.

School was many things, and one thing it was for sure was an extension of the authority of your parents. *"If he gives you any trouble, I want to know about it."* The place was thick with rules and overrun with enforcers from the bus stop to the playground to the classroom. You could be turned in by school patrols, hall monitors, teachers, librarians, lunchroom ladies and even classmates.

You could be stood in a corner, parked in a cloakroom, kept after school or sent to a principal who believed in corporal punishment.

Yes, spanked. Hit so smartly that it felt like backing into a stove and then that same spot hit again and perhaps again so that you whimpered no matter how desperately you tried not to. What if today you spilled coffee at your desk and your boss saw it and called you into his or her office. *"This is not the first time this has happened, Matthews. You have made a mess, distracted others and cost this company money with your carelessness. I have warned you before about this, but now I am going to give you something to help you remember."*

Well, that was part of it and even if there wasn't a last paddling because you managed to avoid suffering the first one, there was, nonetheless, a last time that the prospect of corporal punishment figured in your conduct.

There was a last time:

● You were late to school and the

lonely ping of the flag lanyard against the pole made the desolation of the empty schoolyard complete as you wondered if they would believe the chain-kept-coming-off-my-bicycle story.

● You looked up the answer in the back of the math book and worked backwards to solve the problem, becoming by training an inductive reasoner.

● Frantically waved your arm because you knew the answer and, when it was clear the other kid didn't, kept your arm up, waving it so energetically that you got tired and quickly switched arms, so desperate was your desire to be called on by the teacher who would then love you and commend you to the principal and call your parents, but then she called somebody else.

Remember how funny you felt after all that frantic arm-waving, when the student who was called on gave an answer completely different from yours and it was a good thing you weren't called upon because *you were wrong?*

You were ready to be dropped off at your friend's birthday party insofar that you were bathed, decently dressed and clutching a present that your mom had helped you buy and wrapped herself until she needed you to place your finger on the bow.

When was the last time you pressed your finger on the bow and knew that you were indispensable, that your mother simply would not be able to get along without you?

But you weren't ready for the party, not yet, not by a long shot. Not until your mom had reviewed party manners and satisfied herself that you were not going to embarrass the family by gorging yourself on the biggest piece of cake and then asking for seconds. Mothers live in dread of an incident that might make the morning paper.

CHILD WOLFS DOWN ENTIRE CAKE

FAIRCITY — Sissy Jones, 8, who was old enough to know better, devoured an entire birthday cake and spooned down five gallons of ice cream while neighborhood playmates watched in stunned silence.

Mrs. Estelle Manning, mother of the

birthday child, Kent Manning, 8, said that Sissy not only did not leave any cake or ice cream for anybody else but followed up her gargantuan repast by gobbling all of the jelly beans and nuts out of their pleated paper cups and then popped all of the poppers.

"We expected the little pig to get sick," said Mrs. Manning, "which she did — but not until she had ripped open all of the birthday child's presents. To cap it all off, she left without thanking me or saying that she had a good time."

The hostess wished it to be known that despite the havoc and ruin caused by the Jones child, she in no way blames Sissy. "It was clearly her lack of upbringing. Obviously, her mother, Mrs. Gloria Jones of 112 Elm Drive, is a trashy person, totally lacking in values, who has not troubled to teach her child how to behave in public."

Mothers and fathers, but mothers especially, were sensitive to this kind of feedback. They much preferred the opposite. They loved it when somebody they knew said, "Your Donnie is such a little gentleman when he answers the phone. He takes a message beautifully and he never fails to ask me how I am and to thank me for calling."

The training you received as a youngster was so important to your parents that the job is never quite finished. As much as we revel in last times, we quite understand that even if you are 40 years old, you're going to hear lectures and advice that you've already repeated to your own kids 10,000 times.

So yes, we understand when we ask you when was the last time you were warned to look both ways before crossing the street, it may have been last night by long distance. But chances are you were still begging to stay up to watch "Alfred Hitchcock" when last—

● You were warned never to dig toast out of the toaster because if the fork touched the element even for a billionth of a second you'd be deader than a doornail.

● You were yelled at until you came back in to get a sweater although you had yet to meet anybody who had caught his death of cold.

● Your mom solved the problem of dividing the last piece of pie with your sister by having one child divide and the other choose.

● You were told that if you weren't

sitting yourself down to the supper table at 5:30 with the rest of the family, you weren't getting any.

● You were told "that's a good way to lose a (a) finger, (b) arm, (c) toe, (d) foot (e) tongue."

● You were strongly advised not to wear stripes with checks or plaids.

● You left a sweater or a jacket somewhere and were sent back for it with a reminder of how much it cost. And there was something your mom said as you ran out the door, if we can remember it — how'd that go? "I swear, I do believe you'd lose your . . . " Funny, we can't remember what it was we'd lose if it wasn't fastened to our shoulders. It was right on the tips of our tongues, too.

● You were reminded that there wasn't a money tree growing in the back yard. Variation on same theme: "I'm not made of money, you know."

● You were being a pain in the neck in polite company and your mom secretly tortured you without raising her voice or losing her composure. In olden days moms could crack a skull with a thimble without so much as glancing down or interrupting a conversation. Later, with the passing of lap-sewing and employing

techniques envied by masters of *jujitsu,* they twisted ears, pinched the flesh behind arms and in extreme cases, hooked and turned inside-out lower lips to modify behavior. Do you remember how innocent she looked when you screamed?

● Your mom pinned you with her knees as she reamed out your ears with a washcloth indistinguishable from No. 5 sandpaper, and, despite your squeals of anguish, it was she who acted put upon: "I declare, there's enough dirt in these ears to grow carrots."

● Your mom s-p-e-l-l-e-d in front of you. Later, once you had cracked the code, silence sometimes greeted you when you came into an adult-infested room and someone said, "Little pitchers have big ears." Yes, indeedy, there was a last time you were declared a little pitcher.

● It was more or less suggested that when it came to keeping a bedroom clean and orderly, you and a tornado would finish in a dead heat.

● You were gravely reminded of how badly it would reflect on your home life if you were ever in torn and dirty underwear and run over by a truck. Next chapter, please.

It was someone from Good Samaritan Hospital's emergency room on the line asking for the parent or guardian of Charlotte McAlister.

"I'm Charlotte's mother," Martha McAlister answered frantically. "My God, is she all right?"

"Charlotte's bicycle was hit by a Buick, and, although she is being held for observation, you had better get here right away. The police want to talk to you, but Dr. Hughes wants to see you first."

An hour earlier Charlotte, 16, had left the house to ride to the tennis courts, and even as Martha recalled her daughter's parting a queasy sense of unfinished business gripped her. It was that feeling you get when you're a mile away from the house and wonder if you turned the iron off.

But why? Supper at 6, she had told her daughter that. Don't talk to strangers, be careful, ride with the traffic not against it. Had she neglected anything on the admonition list? What out for the Buicks? No, that was covered by be careful.

Ten minutes later a receptionist sent Martha McAlister into an office where Dr. Eric Hughes nodded, showed her to a chair and shut the door.

"They said she was all right," began Martha. "Can I see . . . "

The surgeon's office-side manner was not convivial. He still wore surgical greens and as he plumped down on a stool opposite Martha, he wiped off his cap, liberating a tumble of dark, sweat-plastered hair.

"Oh, she's ready to go home," Hughes said. "As for her chances of leading a full and meaningful life, I must tell you, Mrs. McAlister, that the prognosis is not rea-suring, not reassuring at all."

"I . . . don't follow you doctor. . . . If she can go home, then it can hardly be brain damage or paralysis, so tell me, what is the problem?"

"There will be charges. Grave charges."

"Because she didn't get out of the way of a Buick? How serious can that be?"

"Mrs. McAlister, this is a most delicate situation and I am not supposed to say anything to you until an investigator gets here, but let me just ask you if you can remember your parting words to your daughter before she left the house on her bicycle?"

"The usual warnings, certainly. Be careful. Avoid strangers. Back in time for supper and of course I cautioned her as I

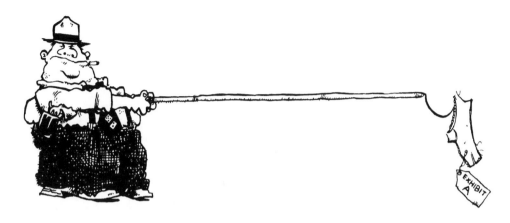

always do to . . . OH NO! I FORGOT! I CAN'T BELIEVE I FORGOT AFTER THE THOUSANDS OF TIMES I WARNED HER NEVER TO LEAVE THE HOUSE IN . . . "

"Torn and dirty underwear, Mrs. McAlister? I must tell you that your dereliction is plainly documented on the report and that the next time you see those torn and dingy Spun-los, they'll be labeled State's Exhibit A."

"Never mind what they do to me, doctor, I don't care. What will happen to Charlotte?"

"She'll never live this down. This tawdry incident will follow her the rest of her days. It is on her record. She will not be admitted to any college, nor permitted to hold a government job or practice law or hold a building contractor's license in any state in the nation. When she moves to a new town she must register her undies with the police."

"Wait just a darned second," exploded Martha McAlister, suddenly lifting her face from her hands. "I just remembered putting those Spun-los on Charlotte's bed this morning. They were freshly laundered and mended."

"I saw the underwear, Mrs. McAlister.

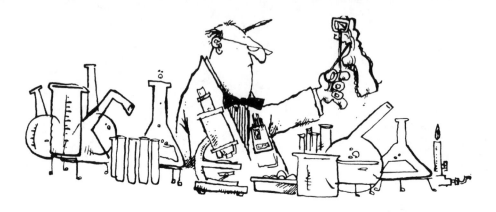

"They were tattletale gray and the elastic was sprung. Don't add perjury to the charges."

"Gray, yes," exulted the mother, "but not dingy. I mistakenly washed them with a blue jumper and I will testify hooked up to a polygraph that they were in perfect condition when Charlotte left the house."

A telephone rang and Hughes answered. "How's that, you say? Clean but traces of dye and the waistband sprung from impact? Thank you, thank you very much."

"Was — was that from the lab?"

Hughes smiled. "You're both in the clear. Go home with a clean record and my heartfelt apology for the misunderstanding."

The matter did not end there, unfortunately. A police reporter picked up the story before it had been corrected and the next day's morning paper assaulted a readership of 200,000 with pictures of the torn and dingy-appearing undergarment under boxcar headlines.

BIKE VICTIM IN TORN AND FILTHY PANTIES — MOTHER SOUGHT.

Retraction and apologies followed, but too late. Even after seven years Martha McAlister hates to answer the telephone because people still call at all hours to chant: "Ring-around-the-waistband."

Giants strode the earth then.

Then being your childhood, the giants grownups. And if it pleases you to remember childhood as a time of laughter and joy and playing after dark in pursuit of lightning bugs, say no more and read no farther.

But let's face it, childhood was spent under house arrest. You didn't own you. Big people were in charge. You went from a womb with no view to a bassinette to a barred crib to a barred playpen, to schools, camps, and a multitude of activities, all supervised, all under perpetual, unrelenting adult control.

You were so supervised that in kindergarten they had something called unsupervised play in which adults stood over you and saw that there was no supervision. There were parents to obey, relatives to kiss, teachers to humor, principals to dread and strangers to avoid.

Through it all you adjusted and matured, lit matches, snuck down to the creek, puffed cigarette butts, used appalling language, ran away from home, lied about homework, looked up dirty words, forged notes, and, sometimes, just because you felt like it, picked flowers for your mother, made your dad a tie rack,

weaved potholders for your grandmother, washed the dishes without being asked and brought a D up to a B.

And in keeping with The Code of Childhood, you never, never, never volunteered to weed the yard.

By the way, when was that last time you were asked to weed the yard? We're guessing here that it followed by two or three years the last time you asked for a pony. Are you old enough to remember "Priscilla's Pop," a newspaper cartoon strip? It was more or less a knockoff of "Little Iodine" and featured a 10-year-old girl who lived in hope that her dad would some day buy her a pony.

We here at this book are persuaded that if there is a metaphysical moment a girl becomes a woman, it is at that instant she not only realizes she is never going to get a pony, but is reconciled to it and looks beyond. That point should be noted and celebrated when she first utters these words:

"Daddy, if I get my driver's license and pay for the extra insurance with my babysitting money . . . "

And in keeping with our conviction that you very well may remember that opening salvo in the propaganda barrage

57

for a car, we are equally convinced that nobody, not even yourself, could possibly freeze-frame that last time you said, "Dad, of course we don't have room here for a horse, but I've checked at the stable and for only $20 a month . . ."

Or for that matter, the last time:

● You were allowed to use the typewriter to hunt and peck your grandmother a letter which began, "How are you, Grandma? I'm fine. Thank you for the . . ."

● You wondered why, since adults are known to carry folding money around with them at all times, they didn't buy four or five Hershey Bars and Baby Ruths a day, and promised yourself that you'd really have a good time when you were rich like that.

● You were warned about taking rides or candy from strangers. Do you recall the horror of hearing that there are crazed adults who will try to get you into the car by saying, "Your mom is hurt at the hospital and she wants you to come with me. Get in." You were reminded about strangers many times, but at some point everybody pretty much agreed that if you didn't know by now, you'd just have to get by on luck.

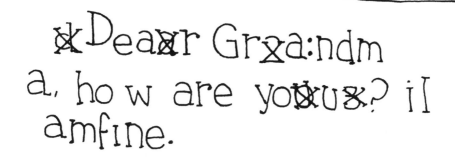

● You were sent home (or to school) with a note safety-pinned to your shirt.

● You were in a crowded place full of adults and you wandered up to your dad, took his hand and were both startled because it was only somebody who looked like your dad from the elbows down.

● You were told on by a snoopy neighbor.

● You had a splinter in your finger and your dad held you down while you thrashed and screeched and otherwise indicated that you'd never hold up under Nazi interrogation and hardly had your dry, racking sobs subsided before he poured a gallon and a half of iodine into the open wound.

● You knew better the next time and went to your mom with the next splinter because she numbed the spot with ice, picked at your splinter with a jeweler's touch, a little at a time and flinched every time you flinched instead of grumbling at you to hold still and stop your belly-aching; and finally, treated the wound mercifully with a dab of mercurochrome.

● You went shell collecting with your grandmother.

● You passed your plate to your mother so she could cut your meat.

Most of us, when we were kids, operated on a bare-bones entertainment budget and became connoisseurs of the cheap thrill. Like when you've blown your only penny on a gumball and the sugary spheroid gets away from you, bounces once and takes off through the checkout line, caroms off a shopping cart wheel and you pounce on it before a fat lady steps on it, that's a cheap thrill.

Not to mention a close call.

And of course, that last gumball round-up happened when you were say, 9 or 10 years old. Now we're not saying you didn't go right on buying gumballs and probably you still do, but at some point in your maturation process you lost sight of the gumball and became infected with dignity. After you were 12 (let's say) and acquired sophistication it was beneath you to chase that rogue gumball, capture it, inspect it for damage and imbedded grit before wiping it on your shirt and popping it into your mouth no matter how many people were looking.

Although we touched on "swing me" earlier, a quick refresher is in order. Swing me is when two adults, one holding each of your hands, hoist you up on the curb, crying "Upsa-daisy" or sometimes "Alley-oop." It was thrilling, offering the same mild upchuck sensation of the elevator dropping out from under you. You'll never be upsa-daisied again.

Do you still try to jump the instant before the elevator drops, hoping to extend that wild moment of free-fall? Are you so rich now that you buy brand new expensive thrills and don't have to rely on cheap thrills?

You've gone wrong somewhere along the way and we need to double back and pick up the trail of what having fun on a zero budget is all about. You came into this world naked but not stripped of accessories. The world was a place of ecstatic tastes, touch, sound, smells and sights. For a year your world was deucedly inconvenient because you lay helpless on your back and waited for everything to come to you.

Once you could crawl and walk and grab, you had it made. If something needed listening to — the dog's asthma, for example — you could go to that dog and tilt your head right against its mouth for the last word in high-fidelity monaural dog breathing. You could taste your way around the yard, bury your face in the dirty clothes hamper, look at a lily until your nose turned yellow.

The first decade of your life was dedicated to taking your body around and

showing it a good time. Remember clenching a marble in your toes and stumping around the house on your heels? Did you ever pretend that you were wounded and practice crawling to the phone in case some day you had to?

We here at this very important book know that when you're with your friends you never say, "Let's go out in the yard and spin around until we get dizzy and fall down." At what age does a person decide he's had enough of lying on his back while the sky spins and he feels like throwing up? Is that why people drink to excess, because they associate feeling dizzy and sick with the happiest times of their lives?

Maybe by concentrating and trying to remember the last time you availed yourself of the cheap thrills of childhood, you can revisit a few of them when nobody else is in the house and there's no danger of the authorities coming and taking you away to an insane asylum. Go back with us now to those golden days of yesteryear when:

● Using powdered sugar, a dab of milk and Bosco chocolate syrup, you made a bowl of icing which you licked off your finger while listening to *Sky King*.

● You weren't too proud to pick up Juicy Fruit® wrappers just to sniff them.

● You built a fort in the woods, a secret fort that nobody else knew about until it occurred to you that nobody would raid it unless you more or less gave directions.

● You sat in a swing while a friend twisted it as far as it would go and let you spin. Had distance jumping contests from a playground swing.

● You spun on a piano stool, experimenting with holding your arms out and then hugging your chest for the twirling ice-skater effect.

● You proved beyond doubt that there are guardian angels by shooting steel-tipped arrows up into the air and not getting stapled to the ground.

● You dragged the dog across the veterinarian's slick tile floor.

● You culled all the black Neccos from the roll while in the lobby so there would be absolutely no chance of accidentally eating one during the double feature.

● You salvaged a burst balloon by sucking and twisting bubbles in the skin and kept on twisting until they popped.

● You "exploded" paper cups in a football stadium. What you do is place a paper cup rim down on a smooth floor and then stomp the cup as smartly as you

can. With perfect technique, the sudden compression produces a pop comparable to a cherry bomb going off.

● Your mom let you stand up on the bus seat so you could pull the bell so the driver would know to let you off at the next stop.

● You played crack-the-whip and got to be the end person and got flung to kingdom come.

● You found change in the washing machine or behind the cushions.

● You waited until someone in your family had gone to a lot of trouble setting up dominos and then prematurely pushed the end domino over and laughed like a loon while you were pummeled half to death by the outraged architect.

● You were so sleepy you were thinking about saying you couldn't go to school because you were sick until suddenly you remembered it was Saturday.

● You stuck a wad of peanut butter on the roof of the dog's mouth and watched him try to dislodge it.

● You gave the pull-cord sign to the semi-truck driver who sounded his horn just for you.

● You were allowed to steer the car.

● Your dad slowed down in the driveway and let you ride the rest of the way on the running-board but only if you didn't tell your mother.

● You sucked a Tootsie Pop® all the way down to the chocolate core, a triumph of will power.

● A friend shared a Three Musketeers® with you without your even asking.

● You talked the teacher into postponing the test until Monday.

● You secretly stashed the last piece of the jigsaw puzzle so you could be the one to put in the last piece. Come to think of it, aren't you the same creep who knocked over the domino? Why you dirty — I

oughta . . .

● You made it to "Go" and instead of having to pay an outrageous $2,000 rent for a hotel on Boardwalk, you got off scot-free and collected $200 to boot.

● You camped out in a tent in the back yard and read comic books with a flashlight.

● You cried because you couldn't learn to yo-yo because the string was too long and when somebody suggested you stand on a chair it worked like a charm.

● You made a friend who was drinking Pepsi-Cola® laugh at just the right moment so that foaming Pepsi gushed out of

his nose.

● You won a butter cookie nibbling contest. To refresh your memory, store-bought butter cookies had scalloped edges and a hole like a donut. To win the nibbling contest, each person had to bite off some cookie without breaking the ring. The ring got skinnier and skinnier until finally . . .

● Your mom rewarded you for going shopping with her by treating you to a vanilla fountain Coke® at Woolworth's. There was something about a Woolworth's lunch counter; they smelled cold like ice cream sodas and hot like homemade soup and were full of the cheery sounds of clinking utensils and trays of sparkling clean glasses being pulled out of steaming washers. The grilled cheese sandwiches were the best anywhere, golden brown and buttery, cut on the diagonal and garnished with dill pickle slices.

Do you miss your cheap thrills? Why? You have them every day. Switching lanes without your tires hitting the reflectors, watching your declawed cat try to climb the curtain, drawing a line through a toll call mistakenly charged to your phone bill, mowing your lawn down to that last tiny patch and then wiping it out, eating the cake away from the icing until you've worked it down to a perfect 1-to-1 icing-cake ratio. . . .

Paper hearts with arrows sticking through them.

There was a last time you made a paper valentine that had a paper arrow sticking through it. That striking three-dimensional effect was somewhat diminished by the arrow's lamentable tendency to tear and droop so that you had to brace it up with cellophane tape. Lots of cellophane tape. Entirely too much cellophane tape.

Yes, and there was a last time during a second week in February when the teacher passed out red construction paper, paper lace, paste and blunt-nosed scissors. Remember those horrible little scissors with the rounded ends? No accident that they were blunt, probably listed in the supplies catalog as "child's anti-impalement scissors." They were useless for gouging your initials in your desk top, but acceptable for self-torture.

What you did for amusement while awaiting instructions was pinch you up some flesh on your hand and then slowly begin to cut it with the scissors, increasing the pressure until you couldn't stand it. This was a popular variation on Fun With Dad's Vise. Or rapping your knuckles with the teeth of a comb and then windmilling your hand to spray droplets of blood.

Gruesome pastimes, to be sure, but not nearly so gruesome as the prospect of making some lacy valentine and giving it in public to the prettiest girl in class who only caught you looking at her 27 times a day. So you made the valentine for your mother and then palmed a handful of candy hearts and dropped them on the pretty girl's desk when no one was looking.

You remember those little hearts with silly messages on them. They were powdery and came in white and pink and blue and said stuff like "Kiss me," "Luv U" and "Be mine." Of course it would be curtains for a guy's reputation to be caught dead with one of those things on his person, so on the side of prudence you might want to clandestinely dump a few cinnamon red hot hearts on her desk and steal into the night or cloakroom, or whatever.

Cloakrooms were fraught with romantic possibilities if only one could figure out how to meet that certain someone there. Alone. And somehow say what's on your mind without strangling on your own drool.

YOU: Oh, it's you. Hi. Do you come into the cloakroom often?

SHE: Yes. I find the smell of damp wool — you'll laugh when I say this —

strangely romantic.

YOU: I love those Rudolph-the-Red-Nosed-Reindeer mittens you're wearing. And by the way, I've loved you from the first day of school.

SHE: We have 12 seconds until the bell. Kiss me.

It was something to think about while cutting out valentines. Girls could snip out valentines of exquisite beauty and full sweeping curves with about two snips. Guys' valentines ended up looking like they had been under the house with the dogs. Our paper hearts were angular and severe, the paper rumpled and the lace pinched and uneven. The "To Mom" came out fine because that was printed on the fat part of the valentine, but on the lower part where you needed more room, you had to scrunch the letters so that they spilled down the edge.

A connoisseur of boys' valentine art could appreciate the dirty clots of paste throughout which generally were gnawed down to the paper and licked to a smooth, professional finish.

With complete premeditation your authors are remembering elementary romance from a boys' point of view because we frankly don't know how it was with you females. We anxiously await word from that quarter. But we do remember

that boys bought the bag of 24 dime store valentines, a fact of commerce with profound sociological implications.

You (half of you then) will remember that there were 32 kids in your class, which meant that eight girls would not get a valentine from each guy. You put your name on the valentine you sent to the other guys, the ones to girls you simply signed "The Phantom." We suspect that girls democratically lopped four roughneck boys and four worst female enemies from their lists.

Try to remember the last time:

● You searched for a gentle way to tell your sweetheart that it was over and a friend suggested telling her (him) "I'm sorry, but the fire is only burning on one side of the forest."

● You were the middleman in a burgeoning romance and your part went something like this: "So-and-so thinks you're cute and is wondering if you think (he or she) is cute."

● You went to a junior high school dance hoping a certain someone would be there. Or don't try to remember and simply read the next chapter and be reminded *exactly* how it was when you were 13, never quite learned to rock and roll and slunk home with your mangled ego in an emotion sickness bag.

"Bye, Mom, thanks for the ride. . . . Yes, Ma'm, you'll pick me up at 11 o'clock in the Hudson."

Right. Eleven o'clock I'll be out front flushed and fevered from 10 minutes of grappling with Henrietta Nesbitt if I can talk her into leaving the dance a few minutes early. Get serious, the only grappling I'll do is with Steve Kesterson for jerking the fruit loop off his Gant® shirt in fifth period today. Besides, how do I know Henrietta's even going to be here?

Better check the money supply. Quarter admission, check; 10 cents for a strawberry Nehi® nickel for a Tom's Peanut Butter Log®, and an emergency dime in case I have to buy the lovely Henrietta Nesbitt a cold drink. And by cleverly keeping a Band-Aid® over mu rubber stamp mark from last week, I'll just . . .uh, oh, pay my quarter and get my other hand stamped because they've gone and changed the black ink to red ink.

Here's Mrs. Philbert with the mimeographed Rec Center Rules of Deportment. Thirty years from now they'll finally figure out that reading blurred purple print causes blindness. Anyway, I know those rules by heart: No food or drink on the dance floor, young ladies and gentle-men will maintain at least one pelvic breadth distance between them during slow dances and no going outside except to neck with the lovely Henrietta Nesbitt. Dream on, Teenage Twirp.

Step into the boys' room, retuck my shirt-tail, darned thing's always puffing out. Comb my hair, roll my sleeves to the deltoids and . . . what in the world — is this gray in my hair? Classic case of Wildroot Cream Oil overload, Charlie, so just comb it out like so, let the excess pile up in the comb gums and wipe the comb on a paper towel.

And now, like Jim Dandy, I'm hip and ready to boot and on the prowl for Henri-etta Nesbitt with the lavender eyes, make that mimeograph purple eyes . . . and . . . and . . . I have this sickening feeling that she's not even here. Crud on a stick! She could be home watching Sgt. Bilko. Or maybe her dirty, filthy, rotten stinking family has packed her up and moved to some stupid place like Oxnard, Califor-nia. My stomach hurts.

Don't get hysterical. She'll be here. After last Friday's dance that was defi-nitely her I saw cruising my house on her bicycle with a girlfriend. I wonder if she

saw me bending open the venetian blinds, scared to come out. Why was I such a chicken-livered coward? I should have simply strolled out for a friendly little chat.

Some friendly chat that would be with three toad-like brothers at my elbow, my mother at the door and my tongue cleaving to the roof of my mouth. Does this boy-girl stuff ever get easy?

Your typical dance floor scene tonight. Guys on one end, girls on the other and a hundred acres of wasted dance floor. Cattle, we look like. No — more like two herds of kangaroos, with a guy popping up every so often to shoot an imaginary two-pointer.

Oh, criminey, they're playing "The Unchained Melody," the only song I can slowdance to and no Henrietta Nesbitt. Henrietta, where are you? Forget swapping gum behind the Rec Center and just be here!

Come on, clown, act your age. There's other fish in the sea. Just go up and ask somebody to dance. Yeah, but they won't dance close like Henrietta did last week and hug me with both arms when The Spaniels sing "Goodnight Sweetheart, Goodnight." Wonder why dancing close

feels so good? It's gotta all be in the mind because when you get right down to it, you're not hugging a girl, you're having a thrilling relationship with 20 layers of crinolines. Miles from girl skin.

A guy if he was smart would invest in a dress form, throw some crinolines on it, put "The Unchained Melody" on the record player and spend weekends locked up in his room. Money ahead in the long run. *"No, Mom, you don't have to drive me to the Rec Center tonight. I'll just stay home and hug my dress form."*

Maybe Henrietta's been here all along and I haven't seen her because her head's buried in some other guy's shoulder. Oh, gosh, my stomach really hurts now. Couldn't blame Henrietta. Guy asks her to dance, what's she gonna do, ask for his vaccination record? I'd just have to cut in, that's all.

But then he'd send a buddy to cut in on me and he'd recut and I'd counter-recut and it would end in nuclear war.

The good news is that I haven't seen Snake Creech here tonight. Snake and his pink suede shoes and skinny white suede belt. He'd be on her like white on rice and making her dance so close that Mrs. Philbert would send for the fire department

83

to hose them down. I can't believe that guy — six-feet-four and in the eighth grade. Henrietta would be powerless. He'd just sweep her up, jam her feet into his pockets and then I'd call him outside to duke it out and then bolt the door behind him and tell Mrs. Philbert to call the police.

Face it, it's almost 9 o'clock and she isn't here. Don't panic. She could be running late. Or car trouble or babysitting toad-like brothers of her own. Or half way to Oxnard. This is what I get for being a chicken-livered coward. All I had to do that day she rode by on her bicycle was go out the door and ask her if she was going to the Rec Center and offer to have my mom pick her up.

What could be simpler or more natural? Repairing a Swiss watch in the dark with a jackhammer comes to mind. I tell you, the guy who figures out a way for a junior high school guy to write a note over the phone is going to make a mint off social mental cases like me.

Crud, it's ladies' choice and they're playing "In the Still of the Night" by the Five Satins and no Henrietta. How do you go about looking available without looking pitiful? There go the non-dancer

guys skulking off for a Nehi® cold drink while the girls pick off the good dancers. Okay, now they're snagging the good-looking guys. There go the tall guys leaving me and the rest of the dregs of Gainesville Junior High School.

So who's the cute girl coming this way? Why the rarest of all creatures, a cute girl actually shorter than yours truly, and if it wasn't for the dumb ducktail haircut, she'd be the spitting image of — holy mackerel! It *is* Henrietta Nesbitt with half her hair cut off! She's been here the whole stupid night!

*"Dance? Sure . . . Say, you were here last week, weren't you? Henrietta, isn't it? Wanna get a Nehi cold drink after this dance? Just happen to have an extra 10 cents here."*

If your early teens were anything like ours, there was a last time you:

● Were driven on a date by your mom and wished you could tell her to take the curves a little faster so your date would lean into you for a cheap thrill.

● Read, or worse, contributed to a "slam book."

● Heard there was a slam book out with your name on it.

● Were sworn to secrecy and crossed

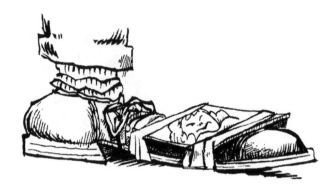

your heart and hoped to die and by rights, should have died within the hour.

● Heard about a friend of a friend who tried the old mirror on the toe of his shoe trick.

● The lights went up, the music stopped and Mrs. Philbert said: "You people look like a mound of octopi out there. Now this close dancing must stop right now or you're all going home. We are young ladies and gentlemen and we will conduct ourselves accordingly. Do I make myself clear? And anyway, I don't understand how you can dance and truly enjoy the music all locked together like that. We will be leaving the lights on. Thank you!" — Everybody: "Awwwwwwwwwwww."

● Went to a TWIRP dance (The Woman Is Requested To Pay).

● Applied Clearasil® and prayed for subdued lighting.

● Heard about people who went out in Nash Ramblers. Wondered what they did if the seats ever stuck down. *"I was showing her how great it would be for camping. . . ."; "She had a headache, so I thought . . ."; "We hit a bump in the road and suddenly the seat . . ."*

We know. Even as you trod nostalgia in our last times, you thought of a zillion more from your own childhood, each more poignant and evocative than anything you saw here.

So let's have them. Come on, right this minute and look at us when we're talking to you . . . What's the matter, cat got your brain?

All bullyragging aside, we do want you to send us your last times. It is not for nothing we came up with *The First Book of Last Times* for the title. Although for convenience we have provided space for five last times, you are welcome to send lots more if you wish.

What's in it for you? Well, your name in print and fame and recognition well within your wildest dreams for openers. For closers, a free copy of *The Second Book of Last Times.*

When was the last time your mom hounded you to write thank-you notes? Try to think of your contributions as a thank-you note. Yes, you can use the typewriter if you're *very* careful and remember to put the cover back on it.

Don't dawdle, and send them to *Last Times,* **300 Sheffield M, West Palm Beach, FL 33417.**

Made in the USA
Charleston, SC
16 March 2011